CONTENTS

Words appearing in the text in bold, **like this**,
are explained in the glossary.

CHEMICALS IN ACTION

What's the link between a violent explosion, a kettle that changes colour when it boils, a melting ice cream, and the leaves of a plant? The answer is materials changes and reactions. They are all examples where substances change to produce new substances. Our knowledge of how materials change and react with each other is used in making chemicals, in medical research, and in engineering.

The study of materials changes and reactions is part of the science of chemistry. Many people think of chemistry as something that scientists study by doing experiments in laboratories with special equipment. This part of chemistry is very important. It is how scientists find out what substances are made of and how they make new materials – but this is only a tiny part of chemistry. Most chemistry happens away from laboratories, in factories and chemical plants. It is used to manufacture an enormous range of items, such as synthetic fibres for fabrics, drugs to treat diseases, explosives for fireworks, **solvents** for paints, and fertilizers for growing crops.

▲ When the chemicals glycerol and potassium permanganate are mixed, the chemical change that happens creates lots of heat.

MATERIAL CHANGES AND REACTIONS

Chris Oxlade

Revised and Updated

www.heinemann.co.uk/library
Visit our website to find out more information about Heinemann Library books.

To order:
 Phone 44 (0) 1865 888112
 Send a fax to 44 (0) 1865 314091
🖥 Visit the Heinemann bookshop at www.heinemann.co.uk/library to browse our catalogue and order online.

First published in Great Britain by Heinemann Library, Halley Court, Jordan Hill, Oxford OX2 8EJ, part of Harcourt Education. Heinemann is a registered trademark of Harcourt Education.

© Harcourt Education Ltd 2003, 2007.
First published in paperback in 2008.
The moral right of the proprietor has been asserted.

Editorial: Clare Lewis
Designed: Steve Mead and Fiona MacColl
Illustrations: Jeff Edwards
Picture Research: Hannah Taylor
Production: Julie Carter

Originated by Modern Age Repro
Printed and bound in China by Leo Paper Group.

10 digit ISBN 0 431 16218 2 (hardback)
13 digit ISBN 978 0 431 16218 8
11 10 09 08 07
10 9 8 7 6 5 4 3 2 1

10 digit ISBN 0 431 16225 5 (paperback)
13 digit ISBN 978 0 431 16225 6
13 12 10 09 08
10 9 8 7 6 5 4 3 2 1

British Library Cataloguing in Publication Data
Oxlade, Chris
    Chemicals in Action: Material Changes and
    Reactions – 2nd Edition
    1. Chemical elements – Juvenile literature
    I. Title
    541.3'9

A full catalogue record for this book is available from the British Library.

Acknowledgements
The Publishers would like to thank the following for permission to reproduce photographs: Alamy Images p24, Andrew Lambert pp18, 21, 28, 36, Bruce Coleman p13, Chris Honeywell p32, Corbis p26, DIY Photo Library p34, Environmental Images p34, Faltner p19, Food Features p8, Hulton Getty p31, Peter Gould pp17, 28 (bottom), Robert Harding p38, Russell Hobbs p5, Science Photo Library pp4, 11, 12, 14, 23, 27, 29, 31, Shout p7, Trevor Clifford pp9, 15, 25, 33, 35, 37, Tudor photography p6.

Cover photograph of a sparkler reproduced with permission of Alamy Images/ Darren Matthews.

The Publishers would like to thank Dr Nigel Saunders for his assistance in the preparation of this book.

Every effort has been made to contact copyright holders of any material reproduced in this book. Any omissions will be rectified in subsequent printings if notice is given to the Publisher.

The paper used to print this book comes from sustainable resources.

About the experiments

There are several experiments for you to try. Doing these will help you to understand some of the chemistry in the book. An experiment is designed to help solve a scientific problem. Scientists use a logical approach to experiments so that they can make conclusions from the results. A scientist first writes down a hypothesis, which he or she thinks might be the answer to the problem, then designs an experiment to test the hypothesis. He or she writes down the results of the experiment and concludes whether or not the results show that the hypothesis is true.

We only know what we do about chemistry because scientists have carefully carried out thousands of experiments over hundreds of years. Experiments have allowed scientists to discover how and why materials change when they are heated or cooled, and how different families of substances react with each other to make new chemicals.

DOING THE EXPERIMENTS

All the experiments in this book have been designed for you to do at home with everyday substances and equipment. They can also be done in the school laboratory. Always follow the safety advice given with each experiment. Ask an adult to help you when the instructions tell you to.

An interesting and fun material change. The whole kettle changes colour to show that the water has boiled.

ABOUT MATERIAL CHANGES AND REACTIONS

In science, the word "material" means any substance around us, from the wood in trees to the air that we breathe. Materials are changing all the time. Just think about the changes that happen in nature throughout the year. During the winter, water can change into ice and snow. In spring, it changes back to water again. Leaves and twigs grow in the spring, then die, and fall from the trees and rot away in the autumn and winter. Solid rocks in the Earth's crust can be changed into soft soil by the action of wind and rain. Now think about the kitchen and the food prepared in it. Ingredients in different foods, such as cakes and breads, change as they are cooked. Runny cake mixture changes into solid cake. The substances change again when you eat and digest them. These are just a few examples of the ways in which materials change.

Material changes happen naturally in plants, animals, and in the Earth itself. We use them to our advantage at home and in many different industries, including the chemical industry. These changes sometimes make the materials look different, feel different, or behave differently. They often make completely new materials that did not exist before.

◀ When you stir sugar into a drink, the crystals of sugar break apart. This is a physical change.

Why changes happen

Material changes do not just happen on their own – there is always a reason for them. In the examples given, water freezes or ice melts because the **temperature** goes down or up. Leaves and twigs rot away because they are eaten by tiny **micro-organisms** in the soil. Food in the oven changes because the temperature is very hot. It changes again when you eat it because it is broken up by your teeth and turned into simpler substances by chemicals in your digestive system.

Fire-fighters trying to stop a fire burning, which is an example of a chemical change.

THE PARTICLE THEORY

Chemists think of substances as being made up of tiny **particles** that are too small to see. This is called the particle theory. These particles are either individual **atoms** or atoms joined together by chemical **bonds** into groups called **molecules**. For example, in a metal all the particles are individual atoms. In water the particles are molecules, each made up of two hydrogen atoms and one oxygen atom. The particle theory helps us to understand how substances behave.

Physical and chemical changes

All material changes are either **physical changes** or **chemical changes**. In a physical change, only the physical **properties** of a material change, its chemical properties stay the same. In a chemical change, the chemical properties change and new materials are formed. The physical properties of the new materials can be completely different to the original materials. Chemical changes are also called chemical reactions.

Imagine a piece of wood. If you cut the wood to make sawdust, it goes through a physical change. It becomes a powder instead of a strong material. Its physical properties have changed, but it is still wood. If you heat the wood instead, it burns and only gas and ashes are left. The wood is no longer wood, so it has gone through a chemical change.

Reversible and permanent changes

Chemical changes are usually permanent, physical changes are not. In a permanent change, the changes made to a material cannot be reversed. Burning wood is an example of a permanent change, because ash cannot be turned back into wood. In a non-permanent or physical change, the change can be reversed. For example, water becomes ice when you put it in the freezer and turns back into water again when you thaw it.

A cake goes through a permanent change in the oven. The cake mixture can never be got back.

EXPERIMENT: EVIDENCE OF REACTIONS

Problem How can we tell that a chemical change is happening?

Hypothesis We can look for signs of a chemical change, such as a change of colour, escaping gas, or heat being made.

EQUIPMENT
- party balloon
- small plastic bottle
- funnel
- vinegar
- baking powder

Experiment steps

1 Push the funnel into the neck of the balloon. Pour a tablespoon of baking powder through the funnel into the balloon.
2 Pour about four teaspoons of vinegar into the bottle. Stretch the neck of the balloon over the neck of the bottle, making sure no powder falls out.
3 Lift up the balloon to make the powder fall into the bottle.

Conclusion

As the powder falls into the vinegar, the balloon inflates. This shows that a gas is made when the powder falls into the vinegar, so a chemical reaction must be taking place.

9

CHANGES OF STATE

Solids, liquids, and gases are called the three states of matter. A change of state occurs when a substance changes from one state to another. For example, when ice (the solid form of water) changes to liquid water, the ice is said to have changed state. Changes of state normally happen when the **temperature** of a substance changes. As the temperature increases, substances change from solid to liquid and from liquid to gas. As the temperature decreases, they change from gas to liquid and from liquid to solid. (There is a fourth state of matter, called plasma, but it is very uncommon.)

All changes of state are **physical changes**. So when a substance changes from one state to another, its physical **properties** change, but its chemical properties stay the same. Changes of state are also reversible changes. This means that when a substance changes state it can change back again. For example, if a piece of metal is heated until it changes state into a liquid, the change will reverse if the liquid metal is cooled.

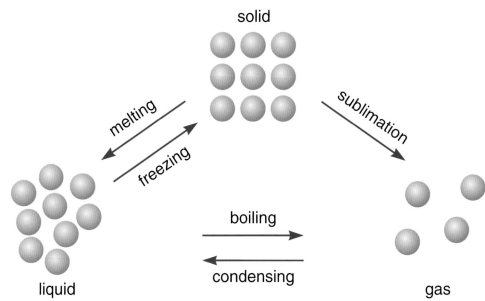

This diagram shows the changes of state from solid to liquid to gas and back again. Sublimation is the change of state from a solid straight to a gas.

Melting and freezing

Melting is the change of state from solid to liquid. A particular substance always melts at a particular temperature, called the substance's **melting point**. For example, the melting point of ice is 0°C (32°F) and the melting point of iron is 1,535°C (2,795°F). Freezing is the change of state from liquid to solid. It is the opposite of melting and it happens as a substance cools. For any substance, the freezing point is the same temperature as the melting point.

Boiling and condensation

Boiling is the change of state from liquid to gas. A particular substance will always boil at a particular temperature, called the substance's **boiling point**. The boiling point of water is 100°C (212°F) and the boiling point of iron is 2,861°C (5,182°F).

Condensation is the change of state from gas to liquid. When a gas is cooled until its temperature reaches its boiling point, it condenses into a liquid.

Evaporation

Evaporation is the change of state from liquid to gas when the liquid's temperature is below its boiling point. The **particles** in a liquid are constantly moving. Sometimes a particle moving upwards at the surface breaks away, escapes into the air, and becomes a gas. Puddles dry up because of evaporation: the water in them slowly escapes to become water **vapour** in the air. The water in the air condenses again if it hits a cold surface.

▶ Some materials, such as solid carbon dioxide, change straight from solid to gas. This change is called sublimation. Solid carbon dioxide is known as "dry ice".

11

Changes of state and particles

Changes of state happen when the **particles** in solids, liquids, and gases either break away from each other or join together. The particles themselves do not change in any way, which is why changes of state are not **chemical changes**.

When a substance is heated so that its **temperature** rises, its particles vibrate more and more. But they stay where they are because the **bonds** between them stay intact. When the temperature reaches the substance's **melting point**, the bonds between the particles begin to break. The particles are now free to move around, so the substance is now in its liquid state. If the liquid cools to below the substance's melting point, the bonds reform and the substance becomes a solid again.

When a substance in its liquid state is heated, its particles move about faster and faster. When the temperature reaches the substance's **boiling point**, the particles break free from each other completely. The liquid has boiled to become a gas. If the gas cools below the substance's boiling point, its particles group together again, bonds reform, and the substance **condenses** to become a liquid again.

◀ White-hot liquid titanium (melting point 1,675°C (3,047°F)) is being poured into a mould to make ingots.

Melting and boiling points

Different substances have different melting and boiling points. For example, water boils at 100°C (212°F), oxygen at -183°C (-297°F), and iron at 2,861°C (5,182°F). A material's melting and boiling points depend on how strong the bonds are between its particles. Materials with weakly joined particles have low melting and boiling points. Materials with strongly joined particles have high melting and boiling points.

More physical changes

Solids, liquids, and gases change in size or in shape as they are stretched or compressed. Solids get slightly longer when you stretch them because the bonds between the particles are stretched. They cannot be easily compressed because the particles are closely packed. The **volume** of a liquid decreases slightly when it is compressed, as the particles are forced closer together. Gases can be compressed much more than solids or liquids, because their particles are widely spread.

Solids, liquids, and gases also change in volume when they are heated or cooled. Solids expand when they are heated, because their particles vibrate more and so take up more space. Liquids expand when they are heated, because their particles move faster and collide more often, and so take up more space. Gases expand when they are heated, because their particles move faster.

Ice is a strange solid because it is less dense than its liquid form, water. This is why it floats.

CHEMICAL REACTIONS

A chemical reaction happens when two or more substances react with each other. After the reaction, one or more new substances have been formed and the original substances have been altered. This means that during a chemical reaction a **chemical change** takes place. The original substances are called the **reactants**, because they react together. The new materials are called **products**.

An example reaction

An example of a common chemical reaction is when gas on a cooking stove burns. The reactants are the gas methane, which comes through the pipes, and oxygen, which is one of the gases in the air. During the reaction two new substances (the products of the reaction) are formed – carbon dioxide, which is a gas, and water **vapour**, which is water in gas form.

The **particles** of oxygen, methane, carbon dioxide, and water vapour are **molecules**. During the reaction, the molecules of oxygen and methane break up and the **atoms** rearrange themselves to form molecules of carbon dioxide and water vapour. The reaction also produces lots of heat energy, which is why we use gas for cooking!

Another reaction

When strips of magnesium are added to hydrochloric **acid**, the magnesium fizzes strongly because the acid reacts with it. This fizzing is made by bubbles of gas forming on the metal. The gas is hydrogen, which is one of the products of the reaction. Another product, called magnesium chloride, is also formed.

Nothing lost, nothing gained

Although reactants disappear and new products appear during a chemical reaction, nothing is lost or gained. All the atoms that are in the reactants are in the products. This means that the total **mass** of the reactants is the same as the total mass of all the products.

Magnesium reacting with hydrochloric acid.

EXPERIMENT: CHANGING SUBSTANCES

Problem

How can we show that reactants change to products in a chemical reaction?

Hypothesis

Burning is a reaction. When a substance burns, the products are gases. If these gases are allowed to escape, then the ash left will be lighter than the object that burned.

EQUIPMENT

- matches and matchbox
- 15 cm (6 inches) ruler
- round pencil
- scissors
- sticky tape

Experiment steps

1 Lay the pencil on a table top and stick it down with sticky tape.
2 Use sticky tape to attach a match to the end of the ruler so the end for lighting hangs over.
3 Balance the ruler on the pencil. Have patience!
4 Ask an adult to help you to light one match and hold it near (but not touching) the match on the ruler until that match lights. Watch what happens.

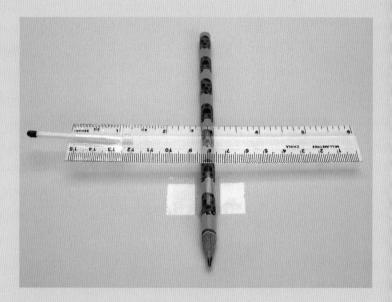

Conclusion

As the match burns, the ruler tips back again, and this shows that the match is lighter after it burns than before. Gases from the reaction must have escaped into the air.

15

Chemical equations

A chemical equation is a way of writing down the changes that happen in a chemical reaction. It shows the **reactants** that take part in a reaction and the **products** that are made during the reaction. The reactants are written on the left side of the equation and the products on the right side. An arrow shows the direction in which the reaction happens; it points from left to right.

Sometimes you will see a double arrow, pointing in both directions. This means the reaction is a reversible reaction, and the products can react with each other to form the original reactants again.

Word equations

In a word equation, the reactants and products are shown by their chemical names. For example, below is the word equation for the reaction between carbon and oxygen. Carbon and oxygen are the reactants and carbon dioxide is the product.

carbon + oxygen	$\rightarrow$	**carbon dioxide**
reactants	**direction of reaction**	**product**

Symbol equations

A symbol equation is an equation in which the reactants and products are represented by their chemical **symbols** and **formulae**. This is the symbol equation for the reaction above:

$C + O_2$	$\rightarrow$	**CO_2**
reactants	**direction of reaction**	**product**

Balanced equations

In a symbol equation, the symbol for each element represents an **atom** of the **element**. Atoms cannot be lost or gained during a reaction, so there must be the same number of atoms of each element on each side of the equation. This is known as a balanced equation.

For example, magnesium and oxygen react to form magnesium oxide. In magnesium oxide, which is a solid, one atom of magnesium always combines with one atom of oxygen. Oxygen gas is made up of **molecules**, each of which contains two oxygen atom. So two atoms of magnesium are needed to react with each oxygen molecule. This is the balanced symbol equation for the reaction:

magnesium   +   oxygen   →   magnesium oxide

$$2Mg \quad + \quad O_2 \quad \rightarrow \quad 2MgO$$

The equation is balanced because there are two magnesium atoms and two oxygen atoms on each side of the equation.

Magnesium ribbon burning. In the reaction, the magnesium combines with oxygen.

Sodium reacts violently with water. The products are hydrogen gas and sodium hydroxide.

Here is another balanced equation, this time for the reaction of sodium and water:

sodium + water   → hydrogen + sodium hydroxide

$$2Na \quad + \quad 2H_2O \quad \rightarrow \quad H_2 \quad + \quad 2NaOH$$

IMPORTANT REACTIONS

Thousands of different chemicals can react with each other, so there are millions of possible chemical reactions. Many reactions are similar to each other, even though the **reactants** and **products** may be different. For example, an **acid** will always react with a metal in the same way. This means that hydrochloric acid reacts with magnesium in the same way that sulfuric acid reacts with zinc. These similarities mean that we can classify chemical reactions into groups that are named after what happens to the reactants during the reaction. The following are groups of reactions that we often see in the laboratory, and that are often used in the chemical industry.

Synthesis

A synthesis reaction is a simple reaction in which two **elements** react together to form a **compound**. For example, if iron filings (which are made up of the element iron) and sulfur are heated together, they react to form iron sulfide:

$$\text{iron} + \text{sulfur} \rightarrow \text{iron sulfide}$$
$$\text{Fe} + \text{S} \rightarrow \text{FeS}$$

Decomposition

A decomposition reaction is one in which a compound splits to make two or more different elements, or more simple compounds. Decomposition often happens when a material is heated – then it is called thermal decomposition. For example, mercury oxide, which is a red powder, decomposes when it is heated. The reaction makes liquid mercury metal and oxygen gas:

Mercury oxide decomposing on heating.

$$\text{mercury oxide} \rightarrow \text{mercury} + \text{oxygen}$$
$$2\text{HgO} \rightarrow 2\text{Hg} + \text{O}_2$$

Neutralization

A neutralization reaction is a reaction of a substance with either an acid or an **alkali**, which turns the acid or alkali into a **neutral solution**. An **acidic** or **alkaline** solution which becomes neutral is said to be neutralized. For example, if sodium hydroxide is gradually added to hydrochloric acid, the acid is neutralized. The products of the reaction are a salt and water:

hydrochloric acid	+	**sodium hydroxide**	$\rightarrow$	**sodium chloride**	+	**water**
HCl	+	NaOH	$\rightarrow$	NaCl	+	H_2O

Most neutralization reactions are used to neutralize acids. Any substance that neutralizes an acid is called a **base**. Magnesium hydroxide is an example of a base. It is used in indigestion tablets, because it neutralizes excess hydrochloric acid in your stomach.

Polymerization

A polymerization reaction is one in which many small, simple **molecules** join together to make a much bigger molecule called a **polymer**. All plastics are polymers.

▲ All these strong, flexible items have been manufactured
from various polymers such as polythene.

Displacement

Sometimes one **element** in a **compound** is replaced by another during a reaction. The first element pushes out, or displaces, the second. This is called a displacement reaction. The most common example is when one metal displaces another metal from a compound. For example, if iron filings are added to a **solution** of copper sulfate (which is blue in colour), the iron displaces the copper. Iron sulfate (which is a brown solid) is formed, along with copper metal:

$$\text{iron} + \text{copper sulfate} \rightarrow \text{iron sulfate} + \text{copper}$$
$$\text{Fe} + \text{CuSO}_4 \rightarrow \text{FeSO}_4 + \text{Cu}$$

One metal displaces another metal in a displacement reaction because the first metal is more reactive than the other metal. This means it can form compounds with other elements more easily than the second metal can.

By writing down which metals displace which others in displacement reactions, you can compile a list of metals in order of how reactive they are (see below). The most reactive metals are at the top and the least reactive at the bottom; this list is called a reactivity series. A metal will be displaced in a reaction by any metal above it in the series.

The reactivity series of common metals. The most reactive metals are at the top and the least reactive at the bottom.

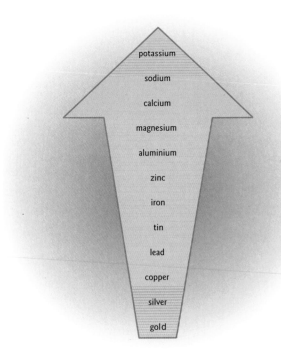

potassium
sodium
calcium
magnesium
aluminium
zinc
iron
tin
lead
copper
silver
gold

A DISPLACEMENT REACTION

How does a displacement reaction happen?

If a solution of a salt that contains one metal is made, and a piece of a metal that is higher in the reactivity series is dropped into it, the first metal should be displaced by the second, more reactive metal.

1 This test tube (right) contains copper sulfate solution. A piece of magnesium ribbon is dropped into the test tube.

2 The magnesium is more reactive than the copper, so it displaces the copper from the solution. Colourless magnesium sulfate is formed, which stays dissolved in the solution. Brown copper metal forms on the magnesium (left).

magnesium + copper sulfate	→	copper + magnesium sulfate
Mg + $CuSO_4$	→	Cu + $MgSO_4$

Oxidation and reduction

An oxidation reaction is any reaction in which oxygen is added to a substance. The **product** of the reaction is normally a substance called an oxide. An oxide is a **compound** made up of an **element** combined with oxygen, such as carbon monoxide or copper oxide. The most common form of oxidation happens when an element combines with oxygen in the air. During oxidation, the substance that combines with oxygen is said to be oxidized. In the reaction below, the magnesium is oxidized because it gains oxygen:

$$\text{magnesium} + \text{oxygen} \rightarrow \text{magnesium oxide}$$
$$2Mg + O_2 \rightarrow 2MgO$$

Reduction

Reduction is the opposite of oxidation. A reduction reaction is any reaction in which oxygen is removed from a substance. During reduction, the substance that loses oxygen is said to be reduced. The thermal decomposition of mercury oxide (see also page 18) is an example of a reduction reaction. The mercury oxide is reduced because it loses oxygen:

$$\text{mercury oxide} \rightarrow \text{mercury} + \text{oxygen}$$
$$2HgO \rightarrow 2Hg + O_2$$

Redox

Redox stands for reduction/oxidation. So a redox reaction is a reaction in which both reduction and oxidation take place. Reduction and oxidation often happen at the same time. During a redox reaction oxygen is removed from one substance and added to another. A redox reaction takes place when hydrogen gas flows over lead oxide. The products of the reaction are lead and water:

$$\text{lead oxide} + \text{hydrogen} \rightarrow \text{lead} + \text{water}$$
$$PbO + H_2 \rightarrow Pb + H_2O$$

Because lead metal is formed, oxygen must have been removed from the lead oxide. The lead oxide has been reduced. At the same time, oxygen has been added to the hydrogen, forming water. The hydrogen has been oxidized.

REDOX IN INDUSTRY

The reaction that takes place inside a blast furnace, where iron is obtained from iron **ore**, is an example of redox at work in industry. Inside the hot furnace, carbon monoxide reacts with the iron ore (which is iron oxide). The iron oxide is reduced, leaving molten iron. The carbon monoxide is oxidized, creating carbon dioxide.

carbon monoxide	+	iron oxide	→	iron	+	carbon dioxide
$3CO$	+	Fe_2O_3	→	$2Fe$	+	$3CO_2$

Electrolysis

Electrolysis is a way of splitting a **compound** using electricity. It works with any substance made up of charged **particles** called **ions**. Negative ions have more **electrons** than **protons**. Positive ions have more protons than electrons. When a substance is in **solution**, or melted, the ions can move.

A circuit is made with a power source and two **electrodes** (electrical conductors) dipped into the substance. One electrode is positive and one is negative. When a current passes through the substance, the negative ions are attracted to the positive electrode and the positive ions are attracted to the negative electrode. At the electrode, the ions lose or gain electrons to become **atoms** with no charge once more.

USING ELECTROLYSIS

Electrolysis has several industrial applications, including metal extraction, electroplating, and electrorefining.

Aluminium is extracted from its **ore**, aluminium oxide, by electrolysis. The aluminium ions in the molten ore move to an electrode, where aluminium metal forms and can be collected. Copper is purified by electrolysis (see picture).

Electroplating is a method of coating a metal object with a layer of another metal. The metal object is used as an electrode during electrolysis. The ions of the metal it attracts form the coating. Tin cans are made from steel with a coating of tin created by electroplating.

EXPERIMENT: ELECTROLYSIS OF WATER

Problem

How can we separate water into oxygen and hydrogen?

Hypothesis

We can try using electrolysis, since some water molecules break up into ions.

EQUIPMENT
- propelling pencil leads or pencil
- clothes peg
- aluminium foil
- battery
- jar or glass

Experiment steps

1. Pour water into the jar until it is 2 cm (1 inch) below the rim.
2. Wrap some aluminium foil around one of the jaws of the clothes peg. Slip the clothes peg over the rim of the jar so that the jaw with the foil is on the inside. Use the peg to clamp two propelling pencil leads to the inside of the jar (the peg should be above the water and the leads should be in it). Alternatively, sharpen a pencil at both ends and clamp this with the clothes peg (make sure that the top end of the pencil lead is in contact with the aluminium foil).

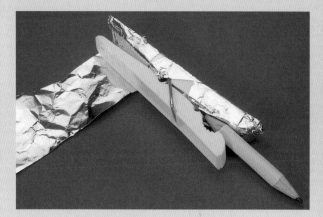

3. Cut a strip of aluminium foil about 20 cm (8 inches) long and 2 cm (1 inch) wide, wrap one end of this around the foil on the jaw but leave about 15 cm (6 inches) free at the other end.
4. Cut a strip of aluminium foil about 30 cm (12 inches) long and 2 cm (1 inch) wide. Push one end of the foil into the water at the opposite end to the clothes peg. Bend it over the rim of the jar, and pass it underneath.
5. Connect the + terminal of the battery to the aluminium foil running from the clothes peg, and connect the – terminal of the battery to the other piece of aluminium foil. Watch what happens.

Conclusion

Bubbles form on the pencil lead and the foil. These two gases must be hydrogen and oxygen – the two **elements** that make up water.

COMMON REACTIONS

On these pages you can find out about some reactions that are happening every day around, and sometimes inside, us! Some of these are vital for the life of plants and animals. Most of them are reactions of materials with oxygen in the air around us. They include combustion, photosynthesis, fermentation, respiration, and corrosion.

Combustion

Combustion, or burning, is the reaction of a substance with oxygen in the air. A combustion reaction always gives out energy – it is an example of an exothermic reaction. "Exothermic" means "gives out heat".

Combustion does not normally start on its own. For example, you need to heat the wick of a candle with a match to light it. This provides the energy to start the reaction, and after that some of the heat from the combustion reaction keeps the reaction going. Lighting the candle is like pushing a ball to get it rolling down a hill – once it gets going, it keeps going.

Because combustion gives off heat and light it is a useful reaction; we burn fuels such as oil, gas, coal, and wood, to provide us with heat and light. A good fuel is one that gives off plenty of energy as it burns. **Fossil fuels**, such as methane (or natural gas), contain carbon and oxygen, and produce carbon dioxide and water when they burn. Combustion is an oxidation reaction because oxygen is added to the substance.

$$\text{methane} + \text{oxygen} \rightarrow \text{carbon dioxide} + \text{water}$$
$$CH_4 + 2O_2 \rightarrow CO_2 + 2H_2O$$

On a cold day you can see gases made by combustion because the water **vapour condenses** in the cold air.

ANTOINE LAVOISIER (1743–1794)

Frenchman Antoine Lavoisier was the first scientist to work out that oxygen from the air combines with a substance when the substance burns. Lavoisier carefully measured the mass of a substance and the **mass** of the **products** after it burned. He found that the mass increased during the reaction. He concluded that a substance must have been added during the reaction, and this substance was oxygen. Lavoisier was also a lawyer and politician. He was executed during the French Revolution because of his wealth.

Fermentation

Fermentation is the reaction in which sugar, such as glucose, is turned to alcohol and carbon dioxide. Fermentation does not happen on its own. It only happens in the presence of a **micro-organism** called yeast. Here is the equation for fermentation:

$$\text{glucose} \rightarrow \text{ethanol} + \text{carbon dioxide}$$
$$C_6H_{12}O_6 \rightarrow 2CH_3CH_2OH + 2CO_2$$

We use fermentation in baking and brewing. In baking, the carbon dioxide released forms bubbles in the dough. This makes the bread rise. In brewing, carbon dioxide makes the alcohol in the drink and the bubbles and froth in beer.

Corrosion

Corrosion is the reaction of a metal with oxygen in the air. It often involves water, too. It turns the metal into a metal oxide, that is much weaker than the metal. The more reactive a metal is the faster it corrodes. Metals at the top of the reactivity series, such as sodium, corrode instantly in the air. Metals at the bottom of the series, such as gold, do not corrode at all. They keep their shine, which is why they are used for jewellery.

The most common form of corrosion is rusting, which is the corrosion of iron and steel. The flaky, red-brown rust is called iron oxide. Here is the equation for the reaction:

$$\text{iron} + \text{oxygen} \rightarrow \text{iron oxide}$$
$$4Fe + 3O_2 \rightarrow 2Fe_2O_3$$

CORROSION OF SODIUM

Sodium is high up the reactivity series, so it corrodes very quickly.

1 A piece of sodium is removed from the oil it is stored in. The oil keeps air and water away from the sodium.

2 The sodium is cut to reveal a fresh metal surface. The surface is observed.

3 The surface very quickly changes colour as the sodium reacts with the air to form sodium oxide. Sodium corrodes very quickly.

Photosynthesis

Photosynthesis is the reaction that takes place in the leaves of plants. Carbon dioxide from the atmosphere and water from the ground react together to make a carbohydrate (sugar). This carbohydrate is the food the plant needs to grow and live.

Photosynthesis needs energy to work. The reaction actually takes in energy, unlike combustion, which gives out energy. It is an example of an endothermic reaction. "Endothermic" means "takes in heat". The energy needed for photosynthesis comes from sunlight that hits the leaves.

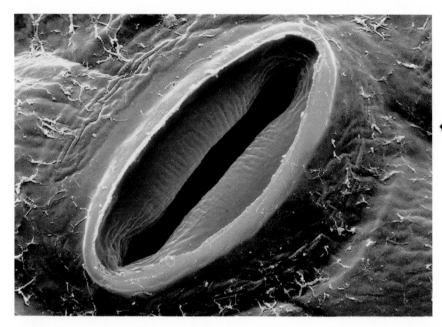

A photomicrograph of the underside of a leaf shows holes called stomata, where carbon dioxide gets in for photosynthesis.

carbon dioxide + water $\rightarrow$ sugar + oxygen

$$6CO_2 + 6H_2O \rightarrow C_6H_{12}O_6 + 6O_2$$

Respiration

Respiration is the opposite of photosynthesis. Sugar and oxygen are turned to carbon dioxide and water. The reaction is exothermic, because it releases energy that animals and plants use to make new chemicals. In animals, the energy is also used for movement.

sugar + oxygen $\rightarrow$ carbon dioxide + water

$$C_6H_{12}O_6 + 6O_2 \rightarrow 6CO_2 + 6H_2O$$

SPEEDS OF REACTIONS

The speed at which a reaction happens is called the rate of reaction. Some reactions naturally happen quickly, while others naturally happen slowly. For example, sodium and dilute hydrochloric **acid** fizz violently because they react very quickly, but iron and dilute hydrochloric acid react together much more slowly. However, the rate of any reaction can be increased in several ways.

More collisions are better

Reactions can only happen when the **particles** of the **reactants** touch each other. So the more chance that the particles have to collide with each other, the faster a reaction will happen. Liquids and gases react together more quickly than solids because their particles can mix easily.

One way to increase the speed of a reaction in which one of the reactants is a solid, is to cut the solid into small pieces. This increases the surface area of the solid so more collisions can happen. For example, the reaction between hydrochloric acid and iron filings is much faster than the reaction between the acid and a block of iron.

Another way of increasing the rate of a reaction is to increase the **temperature** of the reactants. Heat makes their particles move faster, so they collide more often and with more energy. Reactions also go faster if the concentration of a **solution** or the pressure of a gas is increased.

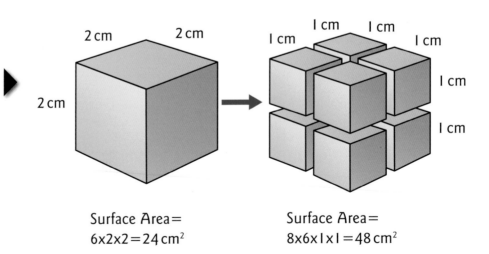

Dividing a piece of a solid into eight pieces doubles its surface area. This would double the rate of a reaction it took part in.

2 cm 2 cm

2 cm

I cm I cm

I cm I cm

I cm

I cm

I cm

Surface Area =
6x2x2 = 24 cm²

Surface Area =
8x6x1x1 = 48 cm²

Catalysts

A **catalyst** is a substance that changes the rate of a reaction. Most catalysts increase the rate of reaction. A catalyst takes part in a reaction, but at the end of the reaction it is the same as it was at the start – it simply helps the process.

Chemical industries use catalysts to help make most of the chemicals they produce, such as plastics, acids, and fertilizers. Using a catalyst often means reactions can take place at room temperature, which saves heating the reactants and using energy. Catalysts also make the reactions more efficient, so that more chemicals can be produced. Rare metals often work as catalysts. For example the catalytic converter in a car's exhaust system uses platinum and rhodium to turn harmful engine gases into harmless ones.

This powder is alumina silica gel, a catalyst used in oil refining.

DANGER IN THE MINES

Coal is mined from under the ground. It is a good fuel, but it has to be heated to a high temperature by firelighters to start it burning, and then it burns quite slowly. Coal dust on the other hand, which is created in mines as the coal is dug out, burns so quickly that it can explode. This is because the dust has a huge surface area. Explosions of coal dust can be set off by tools making tiny sparks, or by lighting a match, and they have caused many mine disasters.

Slowing and stopping reactions

Just as the rate of reaction can be increased, it can also be slowed down or decreased. We often slow the rate of reactions that we do not want to happen. There are also ways of stopping unwanted reactions, such as rusting and burning. For example, there are two ways of slowing down the reactions that make food go off. We can reduce the **temperature** of the food by putting it in a fridge, and add chemicals called additives to the food.

Preventing rusting

Rusting of steel is an expensive problem, so stopping it is important. The easiest way to stop rusting is to cover the steel to stop air and water reaching it. This can be done with paint, plastic, grease, or another metal that will corrode instead of the steel, such as zinc. Covering steel with zinc is called galvanization.

Fighting fires

A fire needs three things to keep it going: fuel, oxygen, and heat. One of these three things must be removed to stop the reaction. For example, fires can be put out by covering them with a blanket or with thick foam from a fire extinguisher, or by putting a burning object under water. All of these remove the supply of oxygen. Heat can be removed by spraying cool water onto a fire. Water cannot be used on electrical fires because it conducts electricity. It cannot be used on oil fires because the oil simply floats on top of the water.

Galvanized (zinc coated) iron dustbins do not rust even when some zinc is scratched off, because the zinc corrodes instead. This is called "sacrificial protection".

EXPERIMENT: PUTTING OUT A CANDLE

Problem

How can we put out a fire?

Hypothesis

One method of putting out a fire is to remove the oxygen that takes part in the combustion reaction.

EQUIPMENT
- short candle
- modelling clay
- old saucer
- glass jar

Experiment steps

1 Stand a candle in the centre of an old saucer, and stop it from toppling over with some modelling clay.
2 Stick a strip of modelling clay around the rim of a jar.
3 Ask an adult to help you light the candle. Once it is burning evenly, turn the jar upside down, over the candle, and press it down to seal the rim. Watch what happens.

Conclusion

After a few seconds the candle goes out, because all the oxygen in the jar has been used up. Burning cannot continue without an oxygen supply. This is how spraying foam on a fire puts it out – it stops the supply of oxygen.

SOLUTIONS

A **solution** is a liquid made when a solid, liquid, or gas dissolves in a liquid. For example, if you stir sugar into water, the sugar dissolves, making a sugar solution. The substance that dissolves to form a solution is called the **solute**. The liquid it dissolves in is called the **solvent**.

When a solute dissolves it seems to disappear, but it does not. Its **particles** mix in with the particles of the solvent. The solution is a mixture of the particles of solvent and particles of the solute. Dissolving is only a **physical change**, not a **chemical change**, because the solute and solvent do not change chemically.

Soluble or insoluble

Water is a very good solvent. Thousands of different substances, such as salt and sugar, dissolve in it. These substances are said to be soluble in water. There are also many substances, such as metals, that do not dissolve in water. They are said to be insoluble in water. Some substances that are insoluble in water, such as oil-based paints, are soluble in other solvents, such as turpentine.

Liquids that dissolve in each other are said to be **miscible**. For example, water and anti-freeze for car engines (which is the chemical ethylene glycol) are miscible. When they are put together, their particles mix completely with each other.

Liquids that do not dissolve in each other are described as **immiscible**. The vinegar and oil that make up salad dressing are immiscible. When they are stirred together, each liquid breaks into small clumps of particles. When the stirring stops, the clumps soon join together again.

Paint strippers are solvents. A chemical in the solvent causes the paint to peel off a surface.

EXPERIMENT: GOOD AND BAD CONDUCTORS

Problem

Does a solute disappear when it dissolves?

Hypothesis

We can tell whether the solute disappears by finding the total weight of the solute and solvent before dissolving, and seeing if the total weight changes when the solute is dissolved in the solvent.

EQUIPMENT
- coat hanger
- string
- two jam jars
- cup (to hold water)
- two teaspoons
- aluminium foil
- salt

Experiment steps

1 Tie a piece of string to the hook of the coat hanger. Use the string to hang the coat hanger from a door handle or similar hook.
2 Tie a piece of string around the neck of each of the jam jars. Use the string to tie a jar to each end of the coat hanger. Make sure the jars hang freely.
3 Half-fill each jar with water. Put a teaspoon into one of the jars, and add water to the other jar until the coat hanger just balances.
4 Cut a square of aluminium foil big enough to cover the top of a jar, and fit it loosely over the jar with the spoon in it.
5 Put two teaspoons of salt on top of the aluminium foil. Carefully add some water to the other jar to balance the coat hanger again.
6 Lift the aluminium foil and pour the salt into the jar. Use the spoon in the jar to stir until the salt dissolves. Leave the spoon in the salty water and put the foil back on top of the jar. What do you notice?

Conclusion

The coat hanger balances again when the salt dissolves in the water. This shows that the total weight of water and salt stays the same, even when the salt has dissolved and cannot be seen any more. So, the salt is still there, it has just broken up into **molecules** too small to see.

Saturated solutions

If you keep stirring salt into a glass of water, there comes a point where no more salt will dissolve. When the water cannot hold any more, we say that the **solution** is a saturated solution. The amount of a **solute** that will dissolve in a particular **solvent** before the solution becomes saturated is called its solubility. Solubility is measured in grams of solute per 100 grams of solvent. For example, the solubility of a salt in water might be 10 grams per 100 grams.

Changing solubility

The solubility of a solute normally changes with **temperature**. For example, the solubility of salt in water goes up as the temperature rises, which means that more salt will dissolve in hot water than cold water.

The solubility of most solids increases as the temperature increases. This means that the higher the temperature, the more solute that is needed to make a saturated solution. The solubility of gases normally decreases as the temperature rises.

A solubility curve is a graph that shows how the solubility of a particular solute in a particular solvent changes with temperature. The solubility is plotted up the vertical axis, and the temperature is plotted along the horizontal axis.

As this saturated copper sulfate solution cools, it cannot hold so much dissolved copper sulfate, which forms crystals.

EXPERIMENT: CHANGING SOLUBILITY

Problem

Does sugar dissolve better in hot or cold water?

Hypothesis

The solubility of solids increases with temperature, so more sugar should dissolve in hot water than in cold water. If a hot sugar solution is allowed to cool down, some sugar will no longer be able to dissolve and crystals of sugar will form.

EQUIPMENT
- pyrex measuring jug
- sugar
- spoon

Experiment steps

1 Ask an adult to heat a kettle of water. The water needs to be hot, but not boiling.

2 Pour out about 100 cm³ (3 fl oz) of the hot water into the measuring jug.

3 Add some sugar and stir to dissolve it. Keep adding sugar until no more will dissolve – it will be very sticky by now! This is a saturated solution of sugar.

4 Leave the sugar solution to cool down and watch what happens.

Conclusion

The solubility of sugar is higher at high temperatures than at low temperatures. This means that a lot more sugar can be dissolved in hot water than in cold water. As the hot sugar solution cools down, the "extra" sugar cannot be dissolved any longer and comes out of the solution as crystals.

ROCK CYCLE AND CHANGES

Over hundreds of millions of years, **physical** and **chemical changes** have happened to the rocks in the Earth's crust to create the landscape we see today.

Types of rock

There are three types of rock in the Earth's crust – **igneous rocks**, **sedimentary rocks**, and **metamorphic rocks**.

Igneous rocks are formed when **molten** rock called magma from deep beneath the Earth's surface cools and sets hard. If it spews from a volcano as lava, the magma cools quickly, and forms dark rock made of tiny crystals. If the magma cools slowly underground, it forms lighter rock with larger crystals.

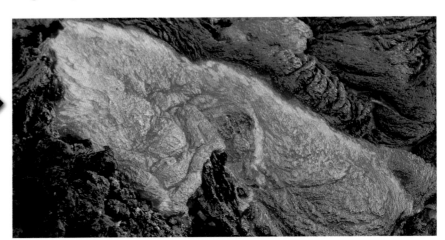

This treacly lava is cooling quickly. When solid, it will form an igneous rock.

Sedimentary rocks are formed when tiny **particles** of rock such as sand settle on the bottom of rivers, seas, and oceans, and form layers. Over time these layers become buried deep underground. The pressure of the layers above eventually squeezes out all the water, and the particles join up to make solid rock. Sedimentary rocks often contain the remains of animals and plants, which are found as fossils. Limestone is a sedimentary rock made up almost completely from the shells of tiny sea creatures.

Metamorphic rocks are formed when the chemical **properties** of igneous rocks and sedimentary rocks are changed by high **temperatures** or by high pressure deep underground. For example, magma flowing into cracks in sedimentary rocks can change the rock next to the cracks into metamorphic rock.

Weathering

Weathering is the wearing away of rocks that are exposed at the Earth's surface. Physical weathering breaks rocks into smaller pieces. The wind creates physical weathering by blowing particles of soil about, which wear away rocks. Water also creates physical weathering by washing loose rock away and carrying it along rivers, where it causes more weathering. Ice creates physical weathering by forming in cracks and splitting rocks apart. Rocks are also weakened as they expand and contract as the temperature around them changes.

Chemical weathering is caused when substances react with rocks and turn them into new substances. For example, **acid** rain reacts with limestone, forming substances that are washed away in the rain water. This slowly eats away the limestone, forming underground caves.

The rock cycle

The rock cycle is the slow circulation of rocks through the Earth's crust, over hundreds of millions of years. For example, weathered rock is washed into the seas, where it forms new sedimentary rocks, while rocks deep underground melt to become magma, which can move back to the surface.

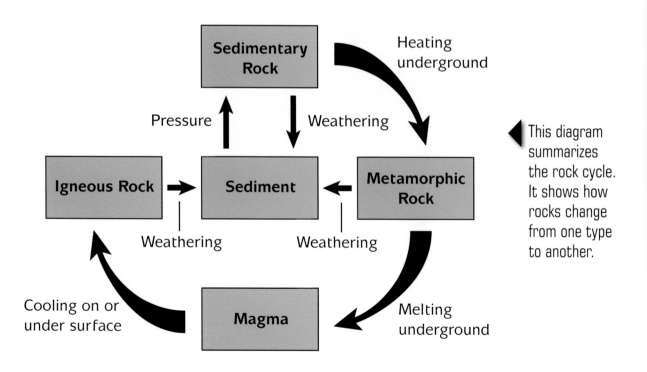

This diagram summarizes the rock cycle. It shows how rocks change from one type to another.

THE PERIODIC TABLE

The periodic table is a chart of all the known **elements**. The elements are arranged in order of their atomic numbers, but in rows, so that elements with similar **properties** are underneath each other. The periodic table gets its name from the fact that the elements' properties repeat themselves every few elements, or periodically. The position of an element in the periodic table gives an idea of what its properties are likely to be.

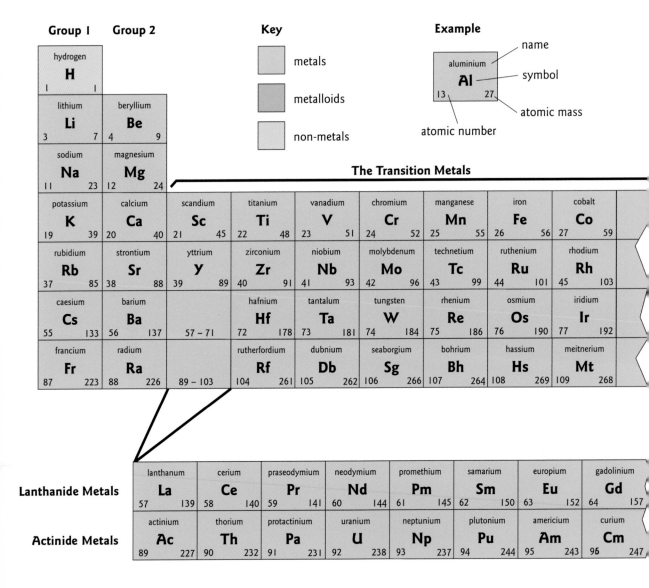

Groups and periods

The vertical columns of elements are called groups. The horizontal rows of elements are called periods. Some groups have special names:

Group 1: **Alkali** metals
Group 2: Alkaline earth metals
Group 7: Halogens
Group 0: Noble gases

The table is divided into two main sections, the metals and non-metals. Between the two are elements that have some properties of metals and some of non-metals. They are called semi-metals or metalloids.

			Group 3	Group 4	Group 5	Group 6	Group 7	Group 0
								helium **He** 2 4
			boron **B** 5 11	carbon **C** 6 12	nitrogen **N** 7 14	oxygen **O** 8 16	fluorine **F** 9 19	neon **Ne** 10 20
			aluminium **Al** 13 27	silicon **Si** 14 28	phosphorus **P** 15 31	sulfur **S** 16 32	chlorine **Cl** 17 35	argon **Ar** 18 40
nickel **Ni** 28 59	copper **Cu** 29 64	zinc **Zn** 30 65	gallium **Ga** 31 70	germanium **Ge** 32 73	arsenic **As** 33 75	selenium **Se** 34 79	bromine **Br** 35 80	krypton **Kr** 36 84
palladium **Pd** 46 106	silver **Ag** 47 108	cadmium **Cd** 48 112	indium **In** 49 115	tin **Sn** 50 119	antimony **Sb** 51 122	tellurium **Te** 52 128	iodine **I** 53 127	xenon **Xe** 54 131
platinum **Pt** 78 195	gold **Au** 79 197	mercury **Hg** 80 201	thallium **Tl** 81 204	lead **Pb** 82 207	bismuth **Bi** 83 209	polonium **Po** 84 209	astatine **At** 85 210	radon **Rn** 86 222
darmstadtium **Ds** 110 281	roentgenium **Rg** 111 272	ununbium **Uub** 112 285	ununtrium **Uut** 113 284	ununquadium **Uuq** 114 289	ununpentium **Uup** 115 288	ununhexium **Uuh** 116 292		

terbium **Tb** 65 159	dysprosium **Dy** 66 163	holmium **Ho** 67 165	erbium **Er** 68 167	thulium **Tm** 69 169	ytterbium **Yb** 70 173	lutetium **Lu** 71 175
berkelium **Bk** 97 247	californium **Cf** 98 251	einsteinium **Es** 99 252	fermium **Fm** 100 257	mendelevium **Md** 101 258	nobelium **No** 102 259	lawrencium **Lr** 103 262

The reactivity series

The reactivity series is a list of common metals in order of their reactivity. The most reactive metals are at the top and least reactive at the bottom. This list gives the reactions of metals with air, water, and acid.

Metal	Symbol	Air	Water	Acid
potassium	K	Burns easily	Reacts with cold water	Violent reaction
sodium	Na	Burns easily	Reacts with cold water	Violent reaction
calcium	Ca	Burns easily	Reacts with cold water	Violent reaction
magnesium	Mg	Burns easily	Reacts with steam	Very reactive
aluminium	Al	Reacts slowly	Reacts with steam	Very reactive
zinc	Zn	Reacts slowly	Reacts with steam	Quite reactive
iron	Fe	Reacts slowly	Reacts with steam	Quite reactive
lead	Pb	Reacts slowly	Reacts slowly with steam	Reacts very slowly
copper	Cu	Reacts slowly	No reaction	No reaction
silver	Ag	No reaction	No reaction	No reaction
gold	Au	No reaction	No reaction	No reaction

PHYSICAL AND CHEMICAL CHANGES

These next two pages summarize **physical** and **chemical changes**.

Physical changes

In a physical change, only the physical **properties** of a material are changed. Its **particles** are rearranged. Its chemical properties remain the same.

Change of state	Change in material
melting	solid to liquid
boiling	liquid to gas
condensation	gas to liquid
freezing (solidifying)	liquid to solid
sublimation	solid to gas

Expansion and contraction
Solids, liquids, and gases expand when they are heated.
They contract when they are cooled.

Changes of shape
Solids change shape when they are compressed, stretched, or twisted.
Liquids and gases flow to take up new shapes. The volume of a liquid decreases slightly when it is compressed. Gases can be compressed easily.

Dissolving
Some solids dissolve when they are put into water or other liquids, making a **solution**. The solid is the **solute**, and the water is the **solvent**.

Chemical changes

In a chemical change or reaction, the chemical properties of materials are changed. The original materials (the **reactants**) are lost, and new materials (**products**) are formed.

Chemical equations
These show the changes that happen during a chemical change.

word equation
magnesium + oxygen → magnesium oxide

symbol equation
$Mg + O_2 \rightarrow MgO$

balanced equation (total atoms on each side are the same)
$2Mg + O_2 \rightarrow 2MgO$

Types of reaction

synthesis
two **elements** combine to form one **compound**, eg:
iron + sulfur → iron sulfide

decomposition
a compound splits up into more simple substances, eg:
mercury oxide → mercury + oxygen

neutralization
an **acid** and a **base** (or **alkali**) react to form a **neutral** solution, eg:
hydrochloric acid + sodium hydroxide → sodium chloride + water

polymerization
two or more **molecules** join together to form a larger molecule
(a **polymer**), eg:
ethene + ethene + ethene ... → polythene

displacement
one element of a compound is replaced by another element, eg:
copper sulfate + magnesium → magnesium sulfate + copper

oxidation
oxygen is added to a substance, eg:
carbon + oxygen → carbon dioxide (carbon is oxidized)

reduction
oxygen is removed from a substance, eg:
mercury oxide → mercury + oxygen (mercury is reduced)

redox reaction
oxidation and reduction happen at the same time, eg:
lead oxide + hydrogen → lead + water (lead is reduced; hydrogen is oxidized)

exothermic
a reaction that gives out heat

endothermic
a reaction that needs heat to work

combustion
a substance reacts with oxygen, giving out heat, eg:
methane + oxygen → carbon dioxide + water

permanent change
the original chemicals can never be got back

reversible change
the change can be reversed to get back the original chemicals

GLOSSARY OF TECHNICAL TERMS

acid liquid that is sour to taste, that can eat away metals, and is neutralized by alkalis and bases. Acids have a pH below 7.

acidic describes a liquid that has a pH below 7. All acids are acidic. Acidic also describes solids or gases that dissolve in water to make acids.

alkali liquid that feels soapy, that is corrosive, and is neutralized by acids. Alkalis have a pH above 7.

alkaline describes a liquid that has a pH above 7. All alkalis are alkaline. Alkaline also describes solids or gases that dissolve in water to make alkalis.

atom extremely tiny particle of matter. An atom is the smallest particle of an element that can exist. All substances are made up of atoms.

base any chemical that neutralizes an acid. Some bases dissolve in water to make alkalis.

boiling point temperature at which a substance changes state from liquid to gas

bond join between two atoms, ions, or molecules

catalyst chemical that makes a chemical reaction happen faster, but is itself unchanged at the end of the reaction

chemical change happens when two chemicals (called the reactants) react together to form new chemicals (called the products)

compound substance that contains two or more different elements joined together by chemical bonds

condensation change of state from a gas to a liquid

electrode solid electrical conductor, usually graphite or metal, that is in contact with the liquid in electrolysis

electron extremely tiny particle that is part of an atom. Electrons are negatively charged, and they move around the nucleus of an atom.

element substance that contains just one type of atom. An element cannot be changed into simpler substances.

formula collection of symbols and numbers that represents an element or compound. It shows what elements are in a compound and the ratio of the numbers of atoms of each element.

fossil fuel fuel formed from the remains of ancient plants and animals. Coal, oil, and gas are fossil fuels.

igneous rock one of the three main types of rock. It is formed when molten rock called magma cools and solidifies.

immiscible describes two liquids that do not mix together, such as oil and water

ion type of particle. An ion is an atom that has lost or gained one or more electrons, giving it an overall positive or negative charge.

mass amount of matter in an object, measured in kilograms

melting point temperature at which a substance changes state from solid to liquid as it warms up

metamorphic rock one of the three main types of rock. It is formed when other rocks are changed by high temperatures and pressures.

micro-orgnanism living thing too small to see without a microscope

miscible describes two liquids that mix together easily

molecule type of particle. A molecule is made up of two or more atoms joined together by chemical bonds. The atoms can be of the same element or different elements.

molten describes the liquid form of a substance that is normally a solid, such as a metal

neutral describes a liquid that is neither an acid nor an alkali. It has a pH of 7. Water is a neutral liquid.

ore material dug from the ground that contains useful elements, such as iron, aluminium, or sulfur

particle very tiny piece of a substance, such as a single atom, ion, or molecule

physical change process in which only the physical properties of a substance change. Changes of state are physical changes.

polymer compound that has molecules made up of lots of small molecules, all the same, joined together in a long chain

product chemical made during a chemical reaction

properties characteristics of a chemical, such as colour, feel, and density

proton one of the particles that makes up the nucleus of an atom. Protons are positively charged.

reactant chemical that takes part in a chemical reaction

sedimentary rock one of the three main types of rock. It is formed when sand or mud falls in layers on the bottom of rivers, seas, and oceans.

solute substance that dissolves in a solvent to make a solution

solution substance made when a solid, gas, or liquid dissolves in a liquid. The substance that dissolves is called the solute and the liquid it dissolves in is called the solvent.

solvent liquid that a substance dissolves in to make a solution

symbol single letter or two letters used to represent an element in chemical formulae and equations

temperature hotness of a substance

vapour gas form of a substance that exists below the substance's boiling point

volume space that something takes up

FURTHER READING

Co-ordinated Science, Chemistry Foundation, Andy Bethell, John Dexter, Mike Griffths (Heinemann, 2001)

e.encyclopedia of science, (Dorling Kindersley, 2004)

The Usborne Illustrated Dictionary of Chemistry, Jane Wertheim, Chris Oxlade, and Dr. John Waterhouse (Usborne, 2006)

The Way Science Works, Jayne Parsons (ed), (Dorling Kindersley, 2004)

Useful websites

http://www.heinemannexplore.com
An online resource for school libraries and classrooms containing articles, investigations, biographies, and activities related to all areas of the science curriculum.

http://www.creative-chemistry.org.uk
An interactive chemistry site including fun practical activities, worksheets, quizzes, puzzles, and more!

www.colorado.edu/physics/2000/periodic_table/index.html
Interactive animation showing the structure of atoms.

http://www.chem4kids.com
Lots of information and activities on chemistry, presented in a fun way.

http://www.webelements.com/webelements/scholar
The Periodic table – online! Discover more about all the elements and their properties.

http://particleadventure.org
An interactive site, explaining the fundamentals of matter and forces!

Disclaimer

INDEX